THE PRESIDENT'S WORK

A LOOK AT THE EXECUTIVE BRANCH

HOW GOVERNMENT WORKS

By Elaine Landau

LERNER PUBLICATIONS COMPANY • MINNEAPOLIS

For Michael Pearl

Lerner Publications Company
A division of Lerner Publishing Group
241 First Avenue North
Minneapolis, MN 55401 U.S.A.

Website address: www.lernerbooks.com

Library of Congress Cataloging-in-Publication Data

Landau, Elaine.
    The President's work: a look at the executive branch / by Elaine Landau.
        p.   cm. — (How government works)
    Includes bibliographical references and index.
    ISBN: 0-8225-0811-7 (lib. bdg. : alk. paper)
    1. Presidents—United States—Juvenile literature. 2. Executive
departments—United States—Juvenile literature. [1. Presidents.
2. Executive departments. 3. United States—Politics and government.]
I. Title. II. Series.
    JK517 .L36 2004
    352.23'0973—dc21   2002010677

Manufactured in the United States of America
1 2 3 4 5 6 – DP – 09 08 07 06 05 04

TABLE OF CONTENTS

INTRODUCTION: LADIES AND GENTLEMEN,
THE PRESIDENT OF THE UNITED STATES....   4

1. BECOMING PRESIDENT   6

2. THE LEADER OF THE FREE WORLD   15

3. THE PRESIDENT AND CONGRESS   22

4. CHIEF EXECUTIVE   29

5. DIRECTOR OF FOREIGN POLICY   37

6. COMMANDER IN CHIEF   42

THE PRESIDENTIAL PATH   48
THE EXECUTIVE BRANCH   49
GLOSSARY   50
SOURCE NOTES   51
BIBLIOGRAPHY   51
FURTHER READING AND WEBSITES   52
INDEX   54

INTRODUCTION: LADIES AND GENTLEMEN, THE PRESIDENT OF THE UNITED STATES....

Usually the president needs no introduction. Everyone knows who that is. Rarely a day goes by without hearing about our nation's leader. We read about the president in newspapers. Or we see the country's chief executive on TV.

The president's work is important to the well-being of our nation. But just what does the president of the United States do? The president plays many roles and has many duties. As chief executive, he or she must make sure that federal laws are enforced. (Federal laws

(Above) John F. Kennedy was one of the first U.S. presidents to use television to address the public.

apply to the whole nation.) As commander in chief of the armed forces, the president must take care of national defense. He or she directs foreign policy, deciding how the United States will relate to other nations. The president suggests laws to members of Congress and tries to get these laws passed. The president is the political leader of his or her political party.

How does the president do all these things? This book tells about the president's work. You will also learn how some presidents have made history. Read on and become a presidential expert. Who knows? Maybe you'll be president someday.

President George W. Bush *(right)* welcomes President Vaclav Havel of the Czech Republic in the Oval Office at the White House on September 18, 2002.

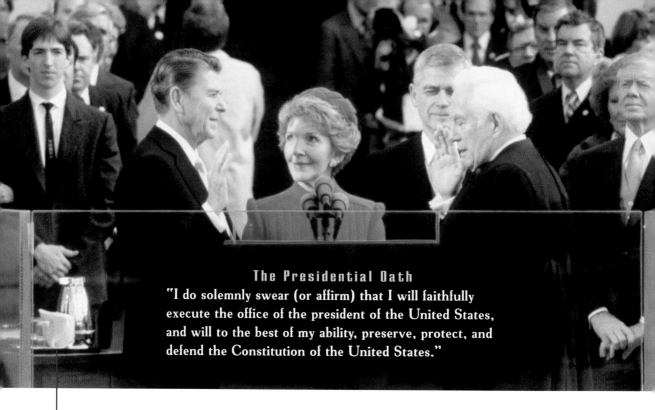

The Presidential Oath
"I do solemnly swear (or affirm) that I will faithfully execute the office of the president of the United States, and will to the best of my ability, preserve, protect, and defend the Constitution of the United States."

CHAPTER 1
BECOMING PRESIDENT

TRUE OR FALSE? Anyone who gets enough votes can become president of the United States. If you answered True to this question, do not skip this chapter. False is the correct answer.

Not just anyone can be president, even if that person is very popular. The Constitution provides only three specific qualifications:

Ronald Reagan *(above, at left)* takes the oath of office for his first term as president on January 20, 1981.

1. You must be a natural-born citizen. That means you were born in the United States.

2. You must have lived in the United States for at least fourteen years.

3. You must be at least thirty-five years old.

Presidents of the United States are elected for terms of four years. The Twenty-second Amendment to the Constitution limits how long a person can be in office. A president can only be elected twice. If a president serves more than two years of another president's term, the rule changes. That person can only be elected once. This may occur when a vice president takes over for a president.

It was not always this way. The Twenty-Second Amendment to the Constitution was passed in 1951. Before that, there was no limit to how many times a president could serve. Franklin D. Roosevelt, the thirty-second president, was an extremely popular president. Roosevelt was elected president four times. Roosevelt did not finish his fourth term, however.

THE YOUNGEST PRESIDENT

John F. Kennedy *(below)*, our thirty-fifth president, was the youngest person ever elected president. He was forty-three when he was elected in 1960. However, Theodore Roosevelt, our twenty-sixth president, became president when he was only forty-two. He had been President William McKinley's vice president. He took office after President McKinley was killed by an assassin in 1901. Roosevelt was later elected to the office at age forty-six.

In 1945 he died while in office, and Vice President Harry S. Truman became the thirty-third president.

ROADS TO THE WHITE HOUSE

Most presidents are elected. But there are other roads to the White House. One is in the Twelfth Amendment to the Constitution. If no presidential candidate wins a majority of the electoral votes after citizens vote, the House of Representatives (the House) chooses the new president. Electoral votes are cast by the electoral college, which is made up of representatives from each state. We've only needed the Twelfth Amendment twice in our history. The House elected both Thomas Jefferson (1801) and John Quincy Adams (1825).

Thomas Jefferson

In 1876 an electoral commission appointed by Congress gave twenty questioned electoral votes to Republican Rutherford B. Hayes. The decision caused Democrat Samuel Tilden to lose the election by one electoral vote. In the 2000 election, the U.S. Supreme Court overruled Florida's Supreme Court in a recount disagreement. This decision gave Florida's electoral votes to Republican George W. Bush, although Democrat Al Gore won the most votes from citizens.

John Quincy Adams

Roads to the White House

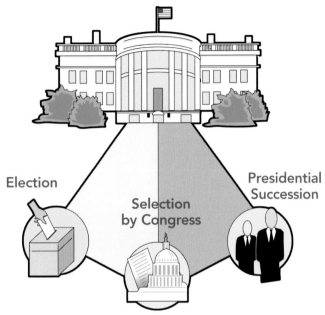

Election

Selection by Congress

Presidential Succession

The Presidential Succession Act of 1947 provides another route to the White House. Usually the vice president takes over if the president dies or is otherwise unable to fulfill the duties. But what if that's not possible? What if the president and the vice president died together in a plane crash, for example? Or what if the president died and the vice president was too ill to take over? Then the Presidential Succession Act of 1947 would go into effect. This law provides a specific order as to who would become president. The first five people are:

1. Speaker (head) of the House of Representatives
2. President pro tempore of the Senate
3. Secretary of State
4. Secretary of the Treasury
5. Secretary of Defense

Franklin D. Roosevelt sits at his desk in the Oval Office in the White House.

All U.S. presidents must take the oath of office, whether newly elected or reelected. Presidents usually take the oath at the inauguration ceremony, which is held at noon on January 20, several weeks after the election.

Presidents take the oath of office very seriously. Many see serving their country as an honor and a privilege. But being president is also a job. Like all government employees, the president is paid. Congress sets the president's salary. It also decides how much money the president will get for staffing, traveling, and care of the White House. That's where the president lives and works. The president receives a yearly salary of four hundred thousand dollars. Presidents cannot give themselves raises, no matter how hard they work.

1600 PENNSYLVANIA AVENUE

The White House is a 132-room mansion. The president lives there with his or her family. They are called the First Family. They live on the second floor. The White House staff lives on the third floor. The president does not have to leave the White House for fun and relaxation. The building has a bowling alley, a movie theater, and even a swimming pool.

Did You KNOW? You could get lost in the White House. It's a big building. The White House has 35 bathrooms, 8 staircases, 12 chimneys, and 147 windows.

The White House has served as the presidential home since 1800.

The White House is much more than just the president's home. It is also an office building. The offices of the president and staff are in a section known as the West Wing. The president's military aides work in the East Wing.

ROADS OUT OF THE WHITE HOUSE

Presidents can be called upon to make important decisions twenty-four hours a day. They often work seven days a week. There are no limits to this job. And a president's performance can affect people around the world.

If people do not think the president is doing a good job, they cannot fire their chief executive. But they can let their voices be heard at the next election. If the president runs for reelection, they can vote for someone else.

The Constitution, however, does provide a way for Congress to remove a president from office. It is a two-part process. First, a majority of the members of the House can impeach, or charge, the president with wrongdoing. For them to do so, the charge must be serious. They must believe that the president has committed acts of "treason, bribery, or other high crimes and misdemeanors."

If the president is impeached, the case goes to the Senate. Then the Senate must try the president on the charges. To remove a president from office, two-thirds of the Senate must vote for conviction.

So far, only two presidents have been impeached—Andrew Johnson, our seventeenth president, and Bill Clinton,

Richard Nixon handed in a letter of resignation *(right)* before his impeachment hearings were complete. The Watergate scandal and Nixon's taped conversations are shown in the spiderweb political cartoon below.

THE WHITE HOUSE
WASHINGTON

August 9, 1974

Dear Mr. Secretary:

I hereby resign the Office of President of the United States.

Sincerely,

Richard Nixon

11.35 AM

HK

The Honorable Henry A. Kissinger
The Secretary of State
Washington, D.C. 20520

our forty-second president. Neither was convicted by the Senate, so both men finished their terms in office.

Richard Nixon, our thirty-seventh president, resigned from office before the House of Representatives could impeach him. He gave up the office on August 9, 1974, due to his involvement in the Watergate scandal. Employees from Nixon's 1972 reelection campaign were convicted of breaking into the Democratic Party's headquarters in the

A Peek at a
PRESIDENT'S CHILDHOOD

Harry S. Truman, the oldest of three children, was born in Lamar, Missouri, in 1884. When he was six years old, his family moved to Independence, Missouri. That's where he attended grade school and high school. That's also where he found out that he was very nearsighted. He had to wear glasses from the time he was eight. Truman was too afraid of breaking his glasses to be active in sports. Instead, he began reading. By his early teens, Truman had read every book in the Independence Public Library. After graduating from high school in 1901, he wanted to go to West Point, a military school in New York State. However, his poor eyesight did not meet the school's standards. Instead Truman attended business school in Kansas City, Missouri.

Watergate building in Washington, D.C. They were searching for information that might help the Republicans win the election. Records of taped White House conversations later revealed that the president came to know of his employees' actions. He had also approved the cover-up of the break-in.

This portrait, taken in 1889, shows Harry Truman at the age of 4 *(right)*, with his two-year-old brother, Vivian.

CHAPTER 2
THE LEADER
OF THE FREE WORLD

QUICK QUESTION: Who is the most important person in the United States?

If you said the president, you are not alone. Much of the world would agree with you. The president of the United States is the leader of a strong and powerful nation.

Many U.S. presidents have been history makers. Their decisions have helped to shape world events. George Washington, Thomas Jefferson, Abraham Lincoln, Theodore Roosevelt,

(Above) President-elect George Washington arrives in New York City—then the capital of the United States—for his inauguration in April 1789.

Woodrow Wilson, Franklin D. Roosevelt, and John F. Kennedy are some of our most respected presidents.

Our nation's founders, often called the Founding Fathers, wanted a strong president. But they wanted their independence too. The president of this new nation had to be a leader who would help all Americans achieve their goals. They did not want a ruler who would force his will on them. The writers of the Constitution were tired of being ruled by kings.

The original Constitution of the United States is displayed in the National Archives Building in Washington, D.C. Every year, more than one million people go there to see it.

CHECKS AND BALANCES

Our nation's founders designed the new government to have three branches—the executive branch, the legislative branch, and the judicial branch. The president is the head of the executive branch. Congress—the Senate and the House of Representatives—make up the legislative branch. The Supreme Court (the nation's highest court)

Did You KNOW? Thomas Jefferson, our third president, wrote the Declaration of Independence in 1776. He remained a firm believer in democracy. Jefferson thought it was better to have too much freedom than not enough.

and other federal courts make up the judicial branch. Each branch operates independently of the others. Power is divided among the branches. This design gives a system of checks and balances. It keeps any one branch from becoming too powerful. That system protects the rights and liberties of all Americans.

For example, Congress has the power to make the nation's laws. The president can veto, or say no to, new laws that Congress wants. But Congress can then override (overrule) presidential vetoes by voting to repass the bill.

The president appoints members of the Supreme Court. But the Senate has to approve the appointments. And the Supreme Court can limit both Congress and the president. The Court decides whether executive actions and laws passed by Congress are constitutional.

The Founding Fathers gathered in Philadelphia in 1787 to write the Constitution. This historical meeting is called the Constitutional Convention.

Congress, which meets in the Capitol *(right)*, and the Supreme Court, which meets in the Supreme Court building *(above)*, both have the ability to check, or limit, the president's power.

Congress limits the president's power in other ways too. For example, the Senate approves or rejects the people the president chooses for important jobs. These jobs include heads of departments and agencies.

THE CHIEF EXECUTIVE

The president heads the executive branch. That is why the president is also called the chief executive. The president's job is huge. That was clear to our nation's founders. They knew that our first president, George Washington, could not do it alone. He would need the advice and help of others.

The Founding Fathers expanded the executive branch. It includes many other people besides the president. The vice president is part of the executive branch. Many departments and agencies are also part of the executive branch.

PEOPLE FILE George Washington, the Father of Our Country, always got a good night's sleep. Parties at the Washingtons' home usually ended early. Mrs. Washington would simply tell guests that the president had to be in bed by nine.

A ball at the White House during George Washington's presidency

They help the president manage the federal government. The heads of these departments assist the president with important issues in specific areas. The department heads are members of the president's cabinet, or board of advisers.

The Department of the Interior is among these departments. It works to protect and conserve our nation's natural resources. It also protects the environment. The department manages millions of acres of land across the nation. This land includes our

DIG DEEPER The president is not just the leader of the country. A president is also the leader of his or her political party. The president campaigns for party candidates and helps raise money for the party.

Theodore Roosevelt was one of the first presidents to champion the environment. He established many national parks during his time in office (1901–1909). Here he is shown as a forest ranger, instructing the public on how to care for our nation's forests.

national parks. You may have visited one of these parks. But you might not have realized that a department in the executive branch of your government protected the area.

In addition, the executive branch includes many independent agencies. These agencies help carry out government programs in different areas. Sometimes these agencies issue rules or provide special services. One such agency is the National Aeronautics and Space Administration (NASA). It is responsible for our space program. Sending an astronaut to the moon or a robotic vehicle to Mars is the work of NASA. So space programs are the work of the executive branch as well.

A Peek at a PRESIDENT'S CHILDHOOD

George Washington was born in Virginia on February 22, 1732. He was the eldest of Augustine and Mary Ball Washington's six children. Unlike most later presidents, Washington did not have much formal education. He probably only went to school for seven or eight years. During that time, he did very well in math. George Washington's father died when George was just eleven. That ended the possibility of his going to school in England like the sons of other landowners. Instead, Washington learned the workings of the family plantation (large farm). Though young, he was hardworking and dependable. His mother relied on him throughout her life.

CHAPTER 3
THE PRESIDENT AND CONGRESS

TRUE OR FALSE? The president of the United States is a powerful person. Therefore, our president can make laws, as long as they are fair and just.

The answer is False. Our chief executive cannot make laws. A president can only recommend legislation, or laws. If a president proposes a bill, an idea he or she hopes will become a law, a member of Congress must submit it. Sometimes the president's cabinet members can help the president get legislation passed.

(Above) Dwight Eisenhower gives his last State of the Union Address (speech) to Congress on January 7, 1960.

They often testify before congressional committees. This lets Congress know what's needed.

WORKING WITH CONGRESS

All presidents want to get their proposed legislation passed. These proposals reflect the policies, or ideas, of the president. In addition to developing policies, presidents also plan a federal budget. This lets Congress know how a president will pay for programs and policies.

Some presidents have been very good at persuading Congress to pass important legislation. Among these presidents was Franklin D. Roosevelt. Roosevelt came to office in 1933. At that time, the nation's economy was in terrible shape.

Did You KNOW? A president's duties include delivering a State of the Union Address (speech) to Congress. The president sums up important issues facing the nation. The address also stresses legislation the president believes is necessary.

This cartoon shows President Lyndon B. Johnson (LBJ) as a bartender at the LBJ Budget Saloon. He is asking two cowboys labeled "Military Establishments" and "Arms Costs" to make room for a little man, labeled "Health, Education and Welfare." In other words, Johnson has to find a way to pay for the military while also paying for schools, medical clinics, and other important services.

Franklin D. Roosevelt created legislation that pulled the American economy out of the Great Depression in the 1930s.

Many businesses, banks, and factories had closed. One out of every four Americans was out of work. Many farmers lost their farms. Lots of people lost their homes. They were unable to pay back their loans. This period in history is known as the Great Depression.

President Roosevelt tried to comfort Americans in his inaugural address. He told the nation, "The only thing we have to fear is fear itself."

SWEEPING LEGISLATION

Roosevelt put together a package of government programs and policies to help people. This plan was known as the

New Deal. Roosevelt persuaded members of Congress to turn his plan into law.

Other presidents have also designed sweeping legislation. Among these is our thirty-sixth president, Lyndon B. Johnson. He was president from 1963 to 1969. Like Franklin D. Roosevelt, Johnson designed laws that helped the poor. One of his national programs was called the War on Poverty.

Johnson also worked for laws to protect the civil rights—basic human rights—of minority groups. He pressured Congress to pass the Civil Rights Act of 1964.

PEOPLE FILE Franklin D. Roosevelt had great personal courage. When he was thirty-nine, he was crippled by polio. Many people thought his political career was over, but he proved them wrong. Roosevelt went on to become one of the nation's most popular presidents.

President Lyndon B. Johnson signing the Civil Rights Act of 1964

This law bans discrimination because of a person's race in businesses that serve the public. It was the most important civil rights bill since the freeing of the slaves after the Civil War.

Andrew Jackson

Not all legislation proposed by presidents has been as noble as the Civil Rights Act, however. Our seventh president, Andrew Jackson, was a well known Indian fighter. He believed that Native Americans and white Americans would never live peacefully together. Jackson wanted to see Indians resettled in a separate part of the nation.

President Jackson strongly supported the Indian Removal Act of 1830. This legislation forced Native Americans who were living east of the Mississippi River to move to land west of the river. Many died during the forced move, known as the Trail of Tears.

PEOPLE FILE As a boy, Andrew Jackson had a hot temper and often got into fights. His mother had wanted him to be a minister. However, she soon saw that he wasn't cut out for it.

THE POWER OF THE VETO

Presidents, however, do more than shape legislation. The president must also approve the laws that Congress passes. First, both houses of Congress (the House of Representatives and the Senate) approve a bill. Then it goes to the president to be signed. If the president is in favor of the bill, he or she signs it.

But a president can also veto a bill. In these cases,

USING THE VETO

Some presidents never used their veto power. These included John Adams, Thomas Jefferson, and Zachary Taylor. In contrast, President Grover Cleveland used his veto power a lot. He vetoed 584 bills. Cleveland was the only president to serve two terms that did not immediately follow each other. He was president from 1885 to 1889. He then won a second term in 1892.

Some presidents have used their veto power more than others. For instance, Andrew Jackson was known for vetoing many bills during his time in office. This cartoon shows Andrew Jackson as the "king" of the United States, wielding his veto power like a weapon.

A Peek at a
PRESIDENT'S CHILDHOOD

Franklin D. Roosevelt was born on January 30, 1882, in Hyde Park, New York. He was the fifth cousin of former president Theodore Roosevelt. Franklin Roosevelt's parents were wealthy and influential, so he grew up with many advantages. He had private tutors. He also went with his parents on many trips to Europe. In some ways, Roosevelt was pampered, but he was not spoiled. His mother taught him to work hard to achieve goals. From his father, the boy learned to care about people who had less than he did.

it is unlikely that the bill will ever become a law. Congress can override a presidential veto, but that doesn't happen very often. Two-thirds of both the House of Representatives and the Senate must vote to repass the bill.

Franklin D. Roosevelt had a privileged childhood. He learned to ride ponies as soon as he was old enough to fit into a saddle.

CHAPTER 4
CHIEF EXECUTIVE

QUESTION: There's a national emergency. Help is urgently needed. Who do our top officials call?

A. The U.S. Marines   B. The police   C. The president

The answer is C. Bet you got that one right. By law, the president has emergency powers— special authority to prevent or deal with a national emergency. The president is also responsible

President Bill Clinton *(above)* comforts a victim of the major floods that hit Iowa in 1993. He declared the floods a national disaster.

for enforcing the laws of the United States. He or she enforces all treaties (written agreements) with foreign nations and all federal court rulings.

THE PRESIDENT'S TOOLBOX

The president has a variety of tools to do all this. One tool is issuing an executive order. An executive order is as powerful as a law. Executive orders do not have to be approved by Congress. Only the president can issue them. The president can also call out the army to enforce a law.

George Washington relied on these tools in 1794 to squelch an event known as the Whiskey Rebellion. Grain is used to make whiskey. In 1791 the government had created a law to tax whiskey. Grain farmers in western

Citizens opposed to the whiskey tax tarred and feathered a government inspector during the Whiskey Rebellion of 1794.

Pennsylvania refused to pay the tax. They armed themselves and marched to Pittsburgh.

In an executive order issued on August 7, 1794, President Washington ordered the farmers to go home. He also called out the army to crush the rebellion. The rebellion was stopped and its leaders arrested. Washington had successfully used the power the president has to enforce the nation's laws.

Many years later, our thirty-fourth president, Dwight D. Eisenhower, again used troops to uphold the law of the land. In 1957 in Little Rock, Arkansas, Governor Orval E. Faubus disobeyed a federal court order. He refused to allow African American students to attend all-white Little Rock Central High School.

On the first day of class, the governor ordered the Arkansas National Guard to surround the school. He said the guard was there to maintain order. Their true purpose, however, was to keep the African American students from entering the school.

A federal judge ordered that the high school be

President Dwight D. Eisenhower

President Bill Clinton *(center)* appointed Norman Mineta *(right)* as his secretary of commerce in 2000.

departments—State, War, and Treasury—and the office of the attorney general. Washington spoke with his department heads often. The modern cabinet has many more departments. Congress adds new ones as needed. The department heads help the chief executive to carry out government policies.

The president often asks for written reports from the department heads. However, the

PEOPLE FILE President Bill Clinton appointed several minority members to his cabinet. In 2000 Clinton selected Norman Mineta as secretary of commerce. Mineta was the first Asian American to hold a cabinet post.

president is not required to take their advice.

The president also appoints judges to federal courts and to the Supreme Court. The Senate must approve the president's choices. Federal courts hear cases involving the Constitution, federal laws, and the U.S. government. The Supreme Court is the highest court in the nation. Its job is to decide whether federal, state, and local governments are acting

Ronald Reagan *(second from right)*, pictured with his family in about 1915

A Peek at a PRESIDENT'S CHILDHOOD

Our fortieth president, Ronald Reagan, was born on February 6, 1911, in Tampico, Illinois. His father was a shoe salesman. His mother was a homemaker. The family moved from town to town in western Illinois as his father looked for work. When Ronald was nine, the Reagans settled in Dixon, Illinois.

Reagan completed elementary school and high school in Dixon. In high school, he took part in football, basketball, track, and swimming. He also appeared in school plays. Later, he became an actor, but there were signs of a political future. He was elected student council president in high school. Reagan graduated in 1928 and went on to Eureka College in Eureka, Illinois.

The THANKSGIVING PARDON

Once a year, the president has some fun with pardons. The president officially recognizes the huge sacrifice made each year by millions of Thanksgiving turkeys. To honor those that give their lives, the president pardons one lucky turkey. That fortunate bird will never spend Thanksgiving on a dinner platter. The day before Thanksgiving, the turkey is sent off to a children's petting farm in Virginia. It spends the rest of its life there. President Harry Truman started this custom. The presidents who followed continued the tradition.

according to the Constitution of the United States.

Besides appointing judges, presidents have other legal powers. They can grant pardons, for example. A person receiving a pardon is forgiven for committing a crime. A president's power to pardon is absolute. The president does not need Senate approval for pardons, and a presidential pardon cannot be overturned.

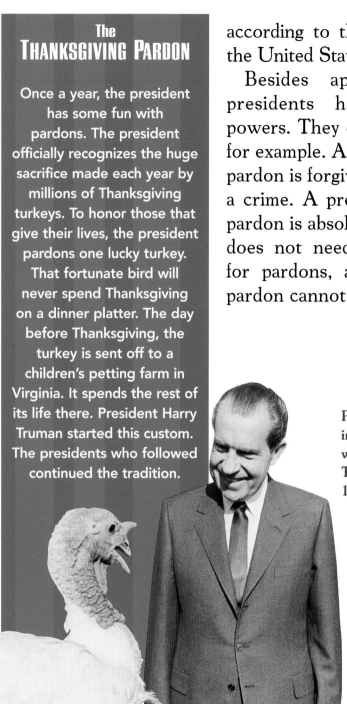

President Richard Nixon, in Washington, D.C., with the pardoned Thanksgiving turkey of 1969

CHAPTER 5
DIRECTOR OF FOREIGN POLICY

TRUE OR FALSE? The president only works on issues concerning the United States. That's why the title is president of the United States and not international premier.

The correct answer is False. Presidents do quite a bit beyond the borders of the United States. The president directs foreign policy. This determines what sort of relationship the United States has with other nations. The secretary of state advises the president on foreign policy.

President Woodrow Wilson *(right)* is pictured with the leaders of Britain, Italy, and France *(left to right)* during peace talks after World War I (1914–1918).

Internatonal RELATIONS

At the end of World War I, President Woodrow Wilson wanted a lasting peace. He led the U.S. delegation to the peace conference in Paris, France. There, he explained his plan for a League of Nations. The league was to be an organization of nations to promote world peace. It was established in Geneva, Switzerland, and lasted from 1920 to 1946. Even with Wilson's hard work, the U.S. Senate rejected the league proposal. The United States was never a member. President Franklin D. Roosevelt also took an active role in foreign policy. He believed that the United States should be a "good neighbor" to the nations of Latin America. Roosevelt was the first U.S. president to visit South America.

But some presidents use their own judgment.

The Constitution gives the president the power to appoint ambassadors. The president also makes treaties. But the Senate has to approve both. An ambassador

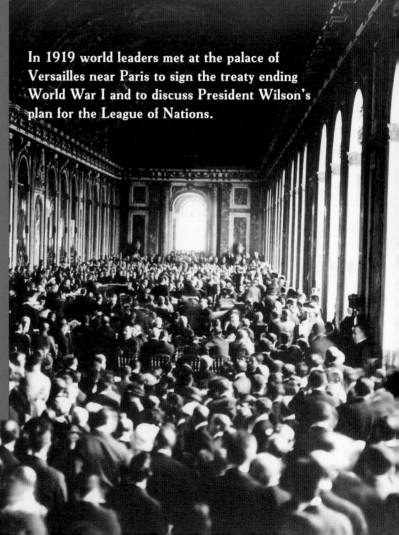

In 1919 world leaders met at the palace of Versailles near Paris to sign the treaty ending World War I and to discuss President Wilson's plan for the League of Nations.

is considered the president's personal representative to another nation. Foreign countries also send ambassadors to the United States.

MAKING TREATIES

When discussing a treaty, the president helps decide what it will say. When all parties agree with its terms, they sign the treaty. In the United States, however, the treaty is not official until the Senate approves it.

President Theodore Roosevelt worked on one treaty that greatly benefited the United States. It involved the Panama Canal. Roosevelt saw the need for a canal connecting the Atlantic and Pacific Oceans. Such a canal would be important for trade and military operations. The canal needed to be built across Panama in Central America. But at the time, Panama was not an independent nation. It was part of Colombia.

"SOUND BYTE" In foreign policy matters, Theodore Roosevelt's motto was to "speak softly and carry a big stick." This means that Roosevelt wanted the United States to take an active leadership role in the world. He believed in having a strong military ("a big stick") to back up our international interests.

In 1902 Roosevelt began working on a canal-building treaty with the Colombians. Then Panama revolted against Colombia and became an independent nation in 1903. Soon afterward, Panama's new government and the United States signed the treaty Roosevelt had wanted. The United States built the canal, which opened in 1914. About 13,500 ships pass through it each year.

Egyptian president Anwar al-Sadat *(left)*, U.S. president Jimmy Carter *(center)*, and Israeli prime minister Menachem Begin *(right)* signing the Camp David Accords in 1979

WORKING TOGETHER

At times, U.S. presidents have served as peacemakers to help other countries work out their differences. Jimmy Carter, our thirty-ninth president, did this in 1978. He helped to make a peace agreement between Egypt and Israel. The two nations adopted the treaty, known as the Camp David Accords, in 1979.

Presidents can often influence foreign policy through foreign aid. For example, a president can suggest how much money the United States will give a foreign country. Congress must pass foreign aid bills. Then the president can sign them or veto them.

A president's foreign policy duties include meeting with ambassadors and leaders from foreign countries. Through the years, U.S. presidents have met with kings, queens, princes, princesses, and many foreign diplomats. Sometimes the president meets with foreign officials in a businesslike setting. At other times, the president has fancy state dinners at the White House. These gatherings are one way countries learn to work together.

Bill Clinton, our nation's forty-second president, met his future wife, Hillary Rodham, while attending Yale Law School.

A Peek at a
PRESIDENT'S CHILDHOOD

Bill Clinton was born on August 19, 1946, in Hope, Arkansas. His father died in a car crash three months before Bill was born. While Bill's mother trained as a nurse in New Orleans, Louisiana, he stayed with his grandparents in Hope. Clinton was influenced by his grandparents' values of religion and education. Bill's mother married Roger Clinton and moved to Hot Springs, Arkansas. Later on, Bill's half brother, Roger Clinton, was born. In high school, Bill played the saxophone and joined student political groups. He earned good grades. He attended Georgetown University in Washington, D.C., then studied at Oxford University in England as a Rhodes scholar. He graduated from Yale Law School in 1973.

CHAPTER 6
COMMANDER IN CHIEF

TRUE OR FALSE? The president has no authority over the armed forces because, unlike some leaders of other countries, the U.S. president does not wear a military uniform.

The answer is False. The president of the United States is the commander in chief of the armed forces. He or she appoints top military officers, but Congress has to approve them. The president can decide to increase or decrease the size

(Above) After the Civil War battle of Antietam in 1862, President Abraham Lincoln *(center)* met with Northern general George McClellan *(sixth from left)*. McClellan was a cautious general, and Lincoln eventually fired him.

of the armed forces and the size of their budget. But, again, Congress has to approve the president's plan.

PRESIDENTS AND THEIR PESKY WARS

The president is responsible for defending the country in time of war and keeping it strong during peacetime. Only Congress can declare war. But presidents can send U.S. troops to fight overseas. They have done so, even when no war has been declared.

On December 7, 1941—during World War II— Japanese war planes attacked the U.S. navy base in Pearl Harbor, Hawaii. The next day, President Franklin D. Roosevelt addressed Congress, asking for a declaration of war. He signed the declaration the same day, and the United States entered the war.

Franklin D. Roosevelt signs the U.S. declaration of war against Japan in 1941.

The United States wasn't at war with Korea when President Truman sent U.S. troops there. On June 25, 1950, the forces of North Korea invaded South Korea. President Truman sent U.S. forces to help the South Koreans defend their country.

Congress supported the president's actions. But the United States never formally declared war against North Korea. Instead the fighting was referred to as a "police action."

"SOUND BYTE" Harry S. Truman had been vice president for just eighty-three days when President Roosevelt died on April 12, 1945. When Truman became president, he told reporters, " I felt like the moon, the stars, and all the planets had fallen on me."

President Harry S. Truman delivers a televised address in the 1950s about the military situation in Korea.

Iranian terrorists paraded their U.S. hostages in front of the U.S. Embassy building in Tehran, Iran, in 1979.

TO THE RESCUE

Military rescues ordered by the commander in chief are not always successful. In 1979 a group of Iranian revolutionaries overthrew the government of Iran. Two weeks later, they took over the U.S. Embassy in Tehran, Iran's capital. The revolutionaries held hostage a group of U.S. citizens—mostly embassy employees.

In April 1980, President Jimmy Carter ordered a military rescue mission to bring the hostages home. Tehran is surrounded by mountains and deserts. About four million people lived in this overcrowded city. It would be difficult to rescue the hostages without harming innocent people.

A U.S. elite Special Operations force was readied for the job. The eight helicopters in the operation were caught in a sandstorm. Three helicopters broke down, and a fourth helicopter accidentally hit a parked U.S. fighter plane. That started a raging fire. Eight people died in the crash, and other crew members were injured.

PEOPLE FILE President Jimmy Carter graduated from the U.S. Naval Academy in Annapolis, Maryland, and served as an officer in the U.S. Navy. He was part of a special group of officers who helped develop the world's first nuclear-powered submarines.

The wreck of one of the eight American helicopters in the failed attempt to rescue American hostages in Tehran in 1980

PRESIDENTIN' AIN'T EASY

Being commander in chief of the armed forces is a big responsibility. The president must carefully weigh risking the lives of Americans against the possible gains. Some presidents have said that sending soldiers to war was the hardest thing they ever had to do.

The president's job is never easy. Only you, your parents, and your teachers see your report card. But the president of the United States is judged by the nation and the rest of the world. American presidents are aware of the importance of their work. Many of the decisions and actions of our presidents have helped preserve our freedom and made our nation great. When you grow up, maybe you'll want the job. Will you have what it takes to be president? Only time will tell.

Young George W. Bush *(left)* with his father

A Peek at a PRESIDENT'S CHILDHOOD

George W. Bush, our forty-third president, was born in New Haven, Connecticut, on July 6, 1946. He was the oldest of six children. When he was two years old, his family moved to Texas, where his father became wealthy in the oil business. In 1959 the Bush family moved to Houston, Texas, where Bush started high school. He was only an average student, but he had a good sense of humor and made friends easily. Bush also played football in high school. George W. Bush finished high school at Phillips Academy, an elite Massachusetts school. In his last year at the school, he headed the football cheerleading team. After graduating, Bush went to Yale University in Connecticut and Harvard Business School in Massachusetts.

The Presidential Path
U. S. Presidents & Dates of Service

1789–1850

George Washington (1789–1797)

John Adams (1797–1801)

Thomas Jefferson (1801–1809)

James Madison (1809–1817)

James Monroe (1817–1825)

John Quincy Adams (1825–1829)

Andrew Jackson (1829–1837)

Martin Van Buren (1837–1841)

William Henry Harrison (1841)

John Tyler (1841–1845)

James Polk (1845–1849)

Zachary Taylor (1849–1850)

1850–1901

Millard Fillmore (1850–1853)

Franklin Pierce (1853–1857)

James Buchanan (1857–1861)

Abraham Lincoln (1861–1865)

Andrew Johnson (1865–1869)

Ulysses S. Grant (1869–1877)

Rutherford B. Hayes (1877–1881)

James A. Garfield (1881)

Chester A. Arthur (1881–1885)

Grover Cleveland (1885–1889)

Benjamin Harrison (1889–1893)

Grover Cleveland (1893–1897)

William McKinley (1897–1901)

1901–2001

Theodore Roosevelt (1901–1909)

William H. Taft (1909–1913)

Woodrow Wilson (1913–1921)

Warren G. Harding (1921–1923)

Calvin Coolidge (1923–1929)

Herbert Hoover (1929–1933)

Franklin D. Roosevelt (1933–1945)

Harry S. Truman (1945–1953)

Dwight D. Eisenhower (1953–1961)

John F. Kennedy (1961–1963)

Lyndon B. Johnson (1963–1969)

Richard M. Nixon (1969–1974)

Gerald R. Ford (1974–1977)

Jimmy Carter (1977–1981)

Ronald Reagan (1981–1989)

George Bush (1989–1993)

Bill Clinton (1993–2001)

George W. Bush (2001–present)

The Executive Branch

This chart shows the basic structure of the federal government and the executive branch in detail.

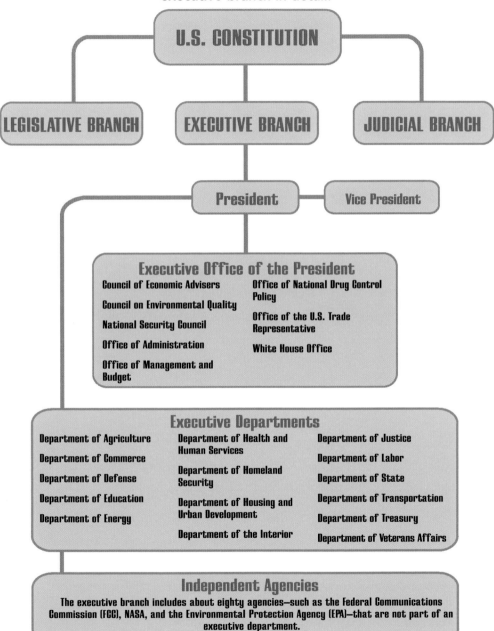

U.S. CONSTITUTION

LEGISLATIVE BRANCH   **EXECUTIVE BRANCH**   **JUDICIAL BRANCH**

President   **Vice President**

Executive Office of the President

Council of Economic Advisers

Council on Environmental Quality

National Security Council

Office of Administration

Office of Management and Budget

Office of National Drug Control Policy

Office of the U.S. Trade Representative

White House Office

Executive Departments

Department of Agriculture

Department of Commerce

Department of Defense

Department of Education

Department of Energy

Department of Health and Human Services

Department of Homeland Security

Department of Housing and Urban Development

Department of the Interior

Department of Justice

Department of Labor

Department of State

Department of Transportation

Department of Treasury

Department of Veterans Affairs

Independent Agencies

The executive branch includes about eighty agencies—such as the Federal Communications Commission (FCC), NASA, and the Environmental Protection Agency (EPA)—that are not part of an executive department.

GLOSSARY

agency: a government organization that provides services to the public

ambassador: a top government official sent to live in and represent a U.S. president in another nation

assassin: a murderer, especially one who kills a government leader

cabinet: the group of presidential advisers who head the executive departments of the president's office

electoral votes: votes cast by the electoral college, which is made up of representatives of each state. They are chosen to elect the president and vice president, based on how voters in each state vote. States have as many electoral votes as they have members of Congress.

executive branch: the branch of government, led by the president, that enforces the laws of the United States

Great Depression: a period in the late 1920s and early 1930s when businesses did poorly and many people lost their jobs

impeach: to officially charge the president or other high official with serious wrongdoing

inauguration: the ceremony at which the president-elect takes the oath of office and officially becomes president of the United States

judicial branch: the branch of our government involving the court system

legislation: laws

legislative branch: the branch of our government that makes laws

pardon: to officially forgive an offense or crime

segregation: the illegal practice of separating people by race

veto: the power a president has to reject a bill that has been passed by Congress in order to keep it from becoming a law

Watergate: the scandal surrounding President Richard Nixon's involvement in the cover-up of the 1972 break-in at Democratic Party headquarters in Washington, D.C.

Source Notes

For quoted material: p. 12, *The Constitution of the United States*, Article II, Section 4; p. 24, Franklin D. Roosevelt, First Inaugural Address, Saturday, March 4, 1933, <http://www.bartleby.com/124/pres49.html>, Accessed November 7, 2002; p. 39, Theodore Roosevelt as quoted by Nathan Miller, *Theodore Roosevelt: A Life* (New York: William Morrow & Co., 1994), 337; p. 44, Harry S. Truman as quoted by Caroline Evensen Lazo, *Harry S. Truman* (Minneapolis: Lerner Publications Co., 2003), 56.

Bibliography

Books

Baldridge, Letitia. *In the Kennedy Style: Magical Evenings in the Kennedy White House*. New York: Doubleday, 1998.

Carter, Jimmy. *An Hour before Daylight: Memories of a Rural Boyhood*. New York: Simon & Schuster, 2001.

Clinton, Hillary Rodham. *An Invitation to the White House*. New York: Simon & Schuster, 1999.

Cornog, Evan, and Richard Whelan. *Hats in the Ring: An Illustrated History of American Presidential Campaigns*. New York: Random House, 2000.

Couch, Ernie. *Presidential Trivia*. Nashville, TN: Rutledge Hill Press, 1996.

Goodwin, Doris Kearns. *Lyndon Johnson and the American Dream*. New York: St. Martin's Press, 1991.

Morris, Edmund. *The Rise of Theodore Roosevelt*. New York: Modern Library, 2001.

Patterson, Bradley H. Jr. *The White House Staff: Inside the West Wing and Beyond*. Washington, D.C.: Brookings Institute, 2000.

Remini, Robert V. *The Life of Andrew Jackson*. New York: HarperPerennial Library, 2001.

Strober, Deborah Hart, and Gerald S. Strober. *Reagan: The Man and His Presidency*. Boston: Houghton Mifflin, 1998.

Periodical and Other Sources

Gallagher, Maria. "The Meal Ticket." *The Philadelphia Inquirer*, August 2, 2000.

Kreisher, Otto. "Desert One." *Airforce Magazine*, January 1999.

The MacNeil/Lehrer Report. Online Newshour, January 21, 1997. <http://www.pbs.org/newshour/@capital/coverage/january97.html>

FURTHER READING

Barber, James G. *Eyewitness: Presidents.* New York: DK Publishing, 2000.

Bausum, Ann. *Our Country's Presidents.* Washington, D.C.: National Geographic Society, 2001.

Cleveland, Will. *Yo, Millard Fillmore! And All Those Other Presidents You Don't Know.* New Milford, CT: Millbrook, 1997.

Davis, Todd, and Marc E. Frey. *The New Big Book of U.S. Presidents: Fascinating Facts about Each and Every President.* Philadelphia: Running Press Book Publishers, 2001.

Debnam, Betty. *A Kid's Guide to the White House.* Kansas City: Andrews McMeel Publishing, 1997.

Dommermuth-Costa, Carol. *Woodrow Wilson.* Minneapolis: Lerner Publications Company, 2003.

Jones, Veda Boyd. *Thomas Jefferson: Author of the Declaration of Independence.* Broomall, PA: Chelsea House, 2000.

Krull, Kathleen. *Lives of the Presidents: Fame, Shame and What the Neighbors Thought.* San Diego, CA: Harcourt, 1998.

Landau, Elaine. *2000 Presidential Election.* New York: Scholastic Library Publishing, 2001.

Márquez, Herón. *George W. Bush.* Minneapolis: Lerner Publications Company, 2002.

———. *Richard M. Nixon.* Minneapolis: Lerner Publications Company, 2003.

Roberts, Jeremy. *Franklin D. Roosevelt.* Minneapolis: Lerner Publications Company, 2003.

Sandler, Martin W. *Presidents.* New York: Harper Collins, 1995.

St. George, Judith. *John and Abigail Adams: An American Love Story.* New York: Holiday, 2001.

———. *So You Want to Be President?* East Rutherford, NJ: Philomel Books, 2000.

WEBSITES

George Washington
Look up this website for a biography of the first president of the United States. Also learn about the country's first First Lady, Martha Dandridge Washington. <http://www.whitehouse.gov/history/presidents/gw1.html>

Inside the White House
Install yourself as president of the United States! Choose your own office furnishings, name the presidential pet, and even check public opinion in the newspapers.
<http://www.pbs.org/weta/whitehouse/whhome.htm>

Life in the Oval Office
Take a tour of the White House's famous Oval Office. While you're there, learn about the history of the most famous office space in the United States.
<http://www.whitehouse.gov/history/life/ovaloffice.html>

Mr. Lincoln's White House
Visit this fascinating website to see what life was like for Lincoln in the White House. Do not miss the virtual tours dealing with important historical events.
<http://www.mrlincolnswhitehouse.org/>

The National Portrait Gallery
See portraits of our presidents. Learn fascinating facts about them in this online tour of portraits.
<http://www.npg.si.edu/exh/travpres/index6.htm>

Presidents' Hall
Visit this informative website to learn the story of each of the presidents. Don't forget to test your presidential knowledge with the Kid's Quiz.
<http://www.whitehouse.gov/history/presidents/>

United States Presidents
Stop here for a brief biography of the presidents of the United States. While you're here, match presidents with their vice presidents.
<http://www.kidsnewsroom.com/elmer/infocentral/frameset/presidents/>

The White House Historical Association
This website is filled with pictures and information for students of all ages. Be sure to try the White House guessing games.
<www.whitehousehistory.org>

The White House for Kids
Check in at the White House website for kids. Learn the "Lessons of Liberty on the Freedom Timeline." Do not miss the photo album with pictures of the White House pets.
<http://www.whitehousekids.gov>

INDEX

Adams, John, 27
Adams, John Quincy, 8
African Americans, 26, 31–32
agencies, 19, 21
ambassadors, 38–39, 41
armed forces, 31–32, 42–44, 45–46, 47
Asian Americans, 34
assassinations, 7

Begin, Menachem, 40
bills, 27–28, 40
branches of government, 16–17
Bush, George W., 5, 8, 47

cabinet, 20, 22–23, 33–34
Camp David Accords, 40
Capitol Building, 18
Carter, Jimmy, 40, 45–46
checks and balances, 17–18
chief executive, 4, 19–20
childhoods of presidents, 14, 21, 28, 35, 41
civil rights, 25–26, 31–32
Civil Rights Act, 25–26
Civil War, 26, 42
Cleveland, Grover, 27
Clinton, Bill, 13, 29, 34, 41
Clinton, Hillary Rodham, 41
Colombia, 39
commander in chief, 5, 42–47
Constitutional Convention, 17

Declaration of Independence, 16
Department of the Interior, 20–21

Eisenhower, Dwight D., 22, 31
elections, 7, 8, 12
electoral votes, 8
emergency powers, 29
environment, 20
executive branch, 16, 19–21

executive departments, 20–21, 33–34, 49
executive orders, 30–32

federal budget, 23, 43
federal courts, 35
federal government, 20, 49
First Family, 11
foreign aid, 40
foreign policy, 5, 37–41
Founding Fathers, 16, 17, 19

Great Depression, 24

Hayes, Rutherford B., 8
hostages, American, in Iran, 45–46

impeachment, 12–13
inauguration, 10, 15
Indian Removal Act, 26

Jackson, Andrew, 26, 27
Jefferson, Thomas, 8, 15–16, 27
Johnson, Andrew, 12–13
Johnson, Lyndon B., 23, 25
judges, 35
judicial branch, 16–17. *See also* U.S. Supreme Court

Kennedy, John F., 4, 7, 16
Korean "war," 44

laws and legislation, 4–5, 9, 17, 22–28, 29–30, 35–36
League of Nations, 38
legislative branch, 16. *See also* U.S. Congress
Lincoln, Abraham, 15–16, 42

McClellan, George, 42
McKinley, William, 7
Mineta, Norman, 34

National Aeronautics and Space
   Administration (NASA), 21
national defense, 5, 43
national emergency, 29
national parks, 20–21
Native Americans, 26
New Deal, 24–25
Nixon, Richard, 13–14, 36

oath of office, 6, 10
Oval Office, 5, 10

Panama Canal, 39
pardons, 36
peacemakers, 38, 40
popular vote, 6, 8
Presidential Succession Act, 9
presidents: ages of, 6, 7; deaths of, 7, 8, 9

qualifications for presidency, 6

Reagan, Ronald, 6, 35
reelection, 10, 12
removal from office, 12
resignation, 12
Roosevelt, Franklin D., 7–8, 16, 23–25, 28,
   38, 43
Roosevelt, Theodore, 7, 15–16, 20, 28, 39
routes to presidency, 8–9

Sadat, Anwar al-, 40
salary, 10
secretary of state, 37
State of the Union Address, 22, 23
Supreme Court Building, 18

Taylor, Zachary, 27
term of presidency, 7–8, 27
Tilden, Samuel, 8
Trail of Tears, 26
treaties, 38–40
Truman, Harry S., 8, 14, 36, 44

U.S. Congress, 5, 10, 12, 16–18, 22–23, 27,
   28, 34, 40, 42–43
U.S. Constitution, 6, 7, 8, 12, 16, 17, 27, 33,
   35, 38, 49; amendments to, 7, 8
U.S. House of Representatives, 8, 12, 13, 16,
   28. *See also* U.S. Congress
U.S. Senate, 12–13, 16, 17, 28, 33, 35, 38, 39.
   See also U.S. Congress
U.S. Supreme Court, 8, 16–17, 18, 35–36

veto power, 17, 27
vice president, 7, 9, 19

war, declaration of, 43
War on Poverty, 25
wars, 42, 43, 47
Washington, George, 15–16, 19, 21, 30–31,
   33–34
Watergate, 12–13
Whiskey Rebellion, 30–31
White House, 5, 10–12, 41
Wilson, Woodrow, 16, 37, 38
World War I, 37, 38
World War II, 43

ABOUT THE AUTHOR

Elaine Landau is a highly acclaimed author of almost two hundred nonfiction books. She has written in many fields, including science, biography, and contemporary issues. Landau has won numerous awards for her work. These awards include: the Best Children's Science Book List from the American Association for the Advancement of Science, Booklist's Top 10 Biographies for Youth, VOYA's Nonfiction Honor List, the New York Public Library Books for the Teenage Citation, and the Children's Book Council's Notable Children's Trade Books in the Field of Social Studies. Landau lives with her family in Miami, Florida.

PHOTO ACKNOWLEDGMENTS

Photographs in this book appear with the permission of: National Archives, pp. 4, 7, 8 (top), 13 (right), 16, 37, 38; © Reuters NewMedia Inc./CORBIS, pp. 5, 34; © Bettmann/CORBIS, pp. 6, 20, 22, 27, 30, 42, 44, 45, 46; Library of Congress, pp. 8 (bottom), 13 (left), 15, 17, 19, 23, 25, 26, 33; Diagrams by Bill Hauser, pp. 9, 49; Franklin D. Roosevelt Library, pp. 10, 24, 28, 43; The White House, p. 11; Harry S. Truman Library, p. 14; Corbis Royalty Free Images, p. 18 (both); © Wally McNamee/CORBIS, pp. 29, 36; Dwight D. Eisenhower Library, p. 31; Arkansas Democrat-Gazette, p. 32; Ronald Reagan Library, p. 35; Jimmy Carter Library, p. 40; © CORBIS SYGMA, p. 41; George Bush Presidential Library, p. 47.

DATE DUE

	NOV 3 0 2010		

FOLLETT